Universe

Universe

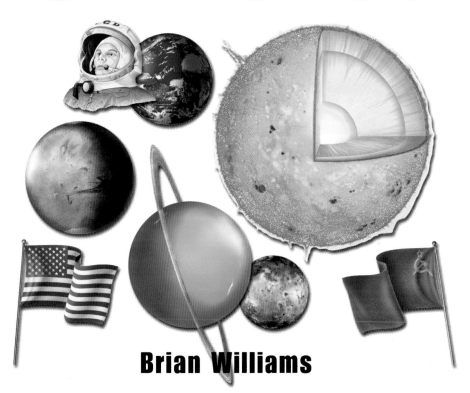

Brian Williams

Miles Kelly
PUBLISHING

Author
Brian Williams

Designed, Edited and Project Managed by
Starry Dog Books

Editor
Belinda Gallagher

Assistant Editor
Mark Darling

Artwork Commissioning
Lesley Cartlidge

Indexer
Janet De Saulles

Art Director
Clare Sleven

Editorial Director
Paula Borton

First published in 2001 by
Miles Kelly Publishing Ltd
The Bardfield Centre
Great Bardfield
Essex CM7 4SL

2468109753

Some material in this book can also be found in *The Greatest Book of the Biggest and Best*

A British Library Cataloguing-in-Publication Data.
A catalogue record for this book is available from the British Library

ISBN 1-84236-025-6
Printed in China

www.mileskelly.net
info@mileskelly.net

CONTENTS

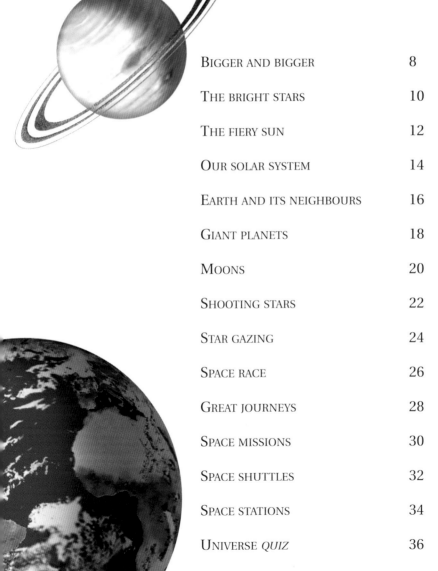

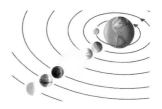

UNIVERSE

The Universe is a pretty difficult subject to comprehend. It is so vast that scientists simply do not know its full extent. The easiest way to describe it is as everything that exists – from the Earth to the Solar System and whatever lies beyond.

Here are thousands of mind-boggling Universe facts that will really fry your brain. For instance, if the Sun was reduced to the size of a football pitch, the Earth would be the size of a pea. And did you know that Jupiter is the biggest planet? In fact Jupiter is so big, that 1,000 Earths would fit inside it.

Explore the biggest and best facts of the *Universe* and unravel some totally cosmic statistics. There are the big, serious facts – for reference – and less serious ones, too, for fun. These pages are packed with some of the biggest and best, oddest and strangest, smallest and funniest, facts around!

BIGGER AND BIGGER

The Universe is the biggest thing there is. Scientists think that it began with an incredible Big Bang – an unimaginably enormous explosion of energy – between 12 and 15 billion years ago. Light from the edge of the Universe takes this long to reach us on Earth. The explosion sent matter flying through space. From this matter the galaxies were formed. Galaxies are great whirling masses of stars. One of those billions of stars is our Sun.

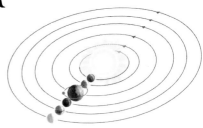

▲ *In 1543 Nicolaus Copernicus proposed a revolutionary theory – that Earth and other planets move around the Sun. Before this people had believed that the Sun and planets moved around the stationary Earth.*

▶ *When the Big Bang happened, it released all the energy in the Universe. As the energy spread out across space, galaxies were formed. The galaxies are still speeding away from each other as the Universe expands.*

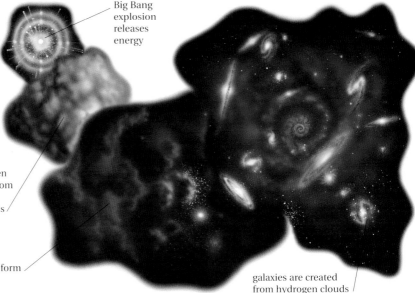

Big Bang explosion releases energy

atoms of hydrogen form as energy from the Big Bang expands outwards

over millions of years massive hydrogen clouds form

galaxies are created from hydrogen clouds

GALAXIES

● The Universe is made up of many millions of galaxies with empty space between them.
● Some galaxies contain as many as 100 billion stars.
● A new star is born in the Milky Way about every 18 days.

▶▶	LIGHT TAKES THIS LONG TO REACH EARTH	
	ORIGIN	**TRAVEL TIME**
★ 1	From the Moon	1.26 seconds
2	From the Sun	8 minutes, 17 seconds
3	From Pluto	5 hours, 20 minutes
4	From the nearest star	4.22 years
5	From the nearest galaxy	150,000 years

spiral galaxy

elliptical galaxy

◀ Some galaxies are elliptical or egg-shaped. Unlike the spiral galaxies, which contain dark, trailing lanes of dust and clouds of gas, elliptical galaxies are huge collections of stars with very little dust or gases. Some elliptical galaxies are much flatter than others when viewed side on.

▲ This is a typical spiral galaxy. Shaped like a catherine wheel, its arms form a thin disc that spiral out from a central bulge. Another type of galaxy is the barred spiral galaxy. Its spiral arms curve away from a bar that crosses the central bulge. Both spiral and barred spiral galaxies contain large amounts of gas and dust as well as stars.

▸▸ GALAXIES VISIBLE WITHOUT A TELESCOPE	
GALAXY	**DISTANCE FROM EARTH**
1 The Large Magellanic Clouds	160,000 light years
2 The Small Magellanic Clouds	180,000 light years
3 The Andromeda Galaxy	2 million light years

◀ The Milky Way is a spiral galaxy, and our Sun is one star among many millions on one of its arms, known as the Orion arm. The biggest galaxy, which is in the Abell 2029 cluster, is 80 times bigger than the Milky Way.

▶ A black hole is all that remains of a collapsed star. You cannot see a black hole. It has such a powerful gravitational pull that not even light can escape from it – so it is invisible. The black hole sucks huge amounts of space matter into a tiny space, making it unbelievably dense – a bit like if Earth was squeezed to the size of a marble.

IT'S A FACT
Stars give out light. Earth's light comes from the Sun. Nothing travels faster than light. A ray of light travels 300,000 km in one second.

THE BRIGHT STARS

There are millions and millions of galaxies, or star-clusters. Each galaxy contains millions of stars. A star is a blazing hot mass of gas, giving off heat and light. The stars are so far away that their light takes years to reach us. The light from the brightest star in the night sky, Sirius, takes almost nine years to reach Earth. Each star is 'born' from a cloud of gas. It grows bigger and hotter, and finally either cools and fades away or explodes like an enormous firework display.

STARS
- Some giant stars give out 50,000 times as much light as the Sun!
- Red stars are the most common stars, but are fairly dim and hard to spot.
- Neutron stars may be only 15 km across.

▶ *Our Sun is a star. It is 150 million km from Earth, and is the closest star to us. The next closest star, Proxima Centauri, is 40 million million km away. The distance between stars is measured in 'light years' – the time it takes for light to travel in one year. Proxima Centauri is 4.22 light years away.*

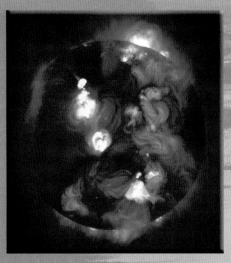

»	HOTTEST STARS	
	STAR TYPE	**TEMPERATURE**
1	Blue	up to 40,000°C
2	Blue-white	11,000°C
3	White	7,500°C
4	Yellow	6,000°C
5	Orange	5,000°C
6	Red	3,500°C

»	BRIGHTEST STARS	
	STAR	**CONSTELLATION**
1	Sirius	Canis Majoris
2	Canopus	Carina
3	Alpha Centauri	Centaurus
4	Arcturus	Bootes
5	Vega	Lyra

▶ *A dramatic way for a star to end its life after shining for millions of years is to explode. This is called a supernova, and is billions of times brighter than the Sun. All that is left is a tiny pulsar, or neutron star.*

▸▸ STARS NEAREST TO EARTH

STAR	DISTANCE FROM EARTH
1 Proxima Centauri	4.22 light years
2 Alpha Centauri	4.35 light years
3 Barnard's Star	5.98 light years

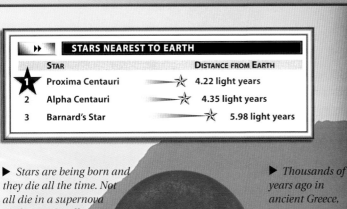

▸ Stars are being born and they die all the time. Not all die in a supernova explosion. Small stars fade away. But before a small star goes out, it expands like a balloon and becomes an enormous red giant one hundred times bigger than the Sun.

▸ A red giant lasts for a few million years. Then the centre of the star begins to shrink and its outer layers are blown away. Finally it becomes a tiny white dwarf like this one, and gradually cools, fades and dies.

▸ Thousands of years ago in ancient Greece, astronomers identified patterns in the groups of stars, called constellations. They gave these patterns the names of heroes or animals, such as Ursa Major, the Great Bear. Scientists have since identified 88 constellations altogether.

Shown here are:
1) Ursa Major
2) Pegasus
3) Hercules
4) Orion
5) Hydra

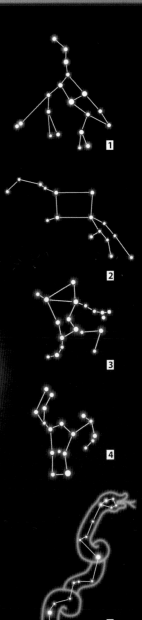

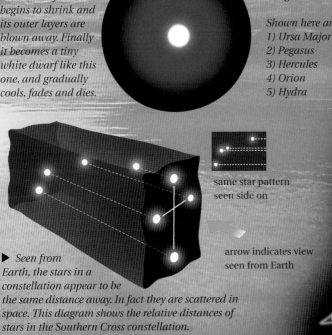

same star pattern seen side on

arrow indicates view seen from Earth

▸ Seen from Earth, the stars in a constellation appear to be the same distance away. In fact they are scattered in space. This diagram shows the relative distances of stars in the Southern Cross constellation.

12 UNIVERSE

» Diameter: 109 times Earth » Hottest part: core » Biggest fireworks: solar prominences » First report of eclipse: 753 BC

THE FIERY SUN

The Sun is one of more than 100 billion stars in the Milky Way galaxy. With other stars, it moves around the centre of the Milky Way galaxy at enormous speed – about 900,000 km/h. It is about 4.6 billion years old, and probably about halfway through its life. The hottest part of the Sun is its core, where temperatures can reach 15 million °C. The Sun is much bigger than Earth, but it is only a middleweight in star terms. The giant star Betelgeuse is 500 times bigger than the Sun!

A LONG WAY TO THE SUN

● The Sun is about 150 million km from Earth. The distance varies as Earth travels around the Sun.

● A spacecraft travelling at the speed of a jet airliner (about 900 km/h) would take nearly 20 years to get to the Sun.

● A spacecraft travelling at 40,000 km/h – the speed needed to escape the pull of Earth's gravity – would take 5 months to reach the Sun.

▲ *A total solar eclipse is a spectacular sight as the Moon covers the face of the Sun. Light from the Sun streams out around the Moon, and on Earth the sky is made dark by the Moon's shadow.*

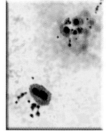

▶ *Sunspots are cooler, dark patches on the Sun's surface. They are caused by changes in the magnetic field within the Sun. Sunspots can be 30,000 km across. The biggest group ever seen, in 1947, was ten times that size! Sunspots increase during an 11-year cycle.*

photosphere

convective zone

◀ *The Sun does not just give us light during the day. At night, light from the Sun is reflected by the Moon, which appears to shine brightly. When Earth passes between the Sun and the full Moon, Earth casts a shadow on the Moon, creating a lunar eclipse.*

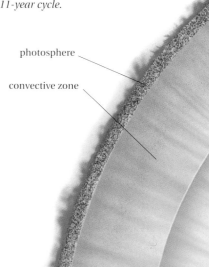

DID YOU KNOW?
All life on Earth depends on energy from the Sun. People in ancient times worshipped the Sun and told stories to explain the rising and setting of the Sun. The Egyptians thought the Sun-god Ra sailed a boat from east to west.

▶ *The Sun sends out long, arching plumes of gas that flare for thousands of kilometres into space. The Sun also gives off strong bursts of radiation that can knock out radio and TV signals and sometimes even power supplies to cities on Earth.*

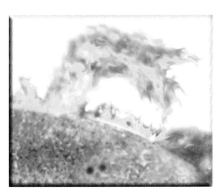

▼ *Earth appears tiny next to the massive Sun. If the Sun were reduced to the size of a football, the relative size of Earth would be no bigger than a pea!*

▼ *The surface of the Sun is called the photosphere. It is about 5,500°C and 300–500 km thick. Beneath lies the turbulent convective zone, at about 1 million °C. Below this active zone is the even hotter radiative zone, at about 2.5 million °C. The core is about 15 million °C.*

core

radiative zone

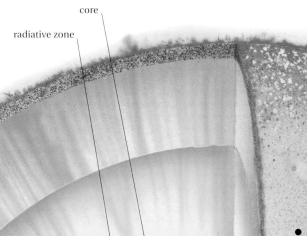

SUN FACTS
- The Sun measures 1,392,500 km across. That is 109 times the diameter of Earth and ten times bigger than Jupiter.
- The Sun is 330,000 times heavier than Earth. Its volume, the amount of matter in it, is roughly 1.3 million times bigger than Earth's.
- The Sun is 400 times farther away from us than the Moon.

Our Solar System

After the Sun was formed from a great cloud of gas, lots of matter was left over. This whirled around the new star, in time forming a system of nine planets, which we call the Solar System. The four planets closest to the Sun are small and rocky. The four much larger outer planets are made of liquid gas and ice. The outermost planet, Pluto, is the smallest. There may be another small planet beyond Pluto.

» PLANET EXTREMES

Hottest	Venus	462°C
Coldest	Pluto	About -235°C
Fastest	Mercury	172,000 km/h
Faintest	Pluto	Visible only by telescope
Densest	Earth	5x water

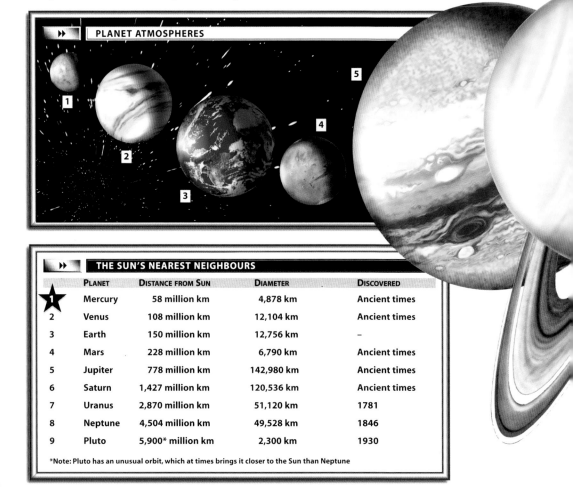

» PLANET ATMOSPHERES

» THE SUN'S NEAREST NEIGHBOURS

	PLANET	DISTANCE FROM SUN	DIAMETER	DISCOVERED
1	Mercury	58 million km	4,878 km	Ancient times
2	Venus	108 million km	12,104 km	Ancient times
3	Earth	150 million km	12,756 km	–
4	Mars	228 million km	6,790 km	Ancient times
5	Jupiter	778 million km	142,980 km	Ancient times
6	Saturn	1,427 million km	120,536 km	Ancient times
7	Uranus	2,870 million km	51,120 km	1781
8	Neptune	4,504 million km	49,528 km	1846
9	Pluto	5,900* million km	2,300 km	1930

*Note: Pluto has an unusual orbit, which at times brings it closer to the Sun than Neptune

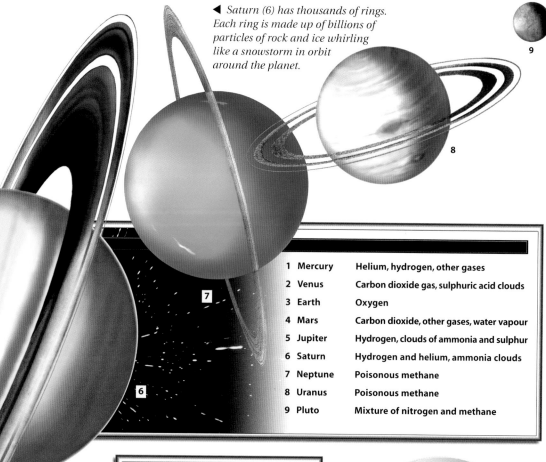

◀ *Saturn (6) has thousands of rings.*
Each ring is made up of billions of
particles of rock and ice whirling
like a snowstorm in orbit
around the planet.

1	Mercury	Helium, hydrogen, other gases
2	Venus	Carbon dioxide gas, sulphuric acid clouds
3	Earth	Oxygen
4	Mars	Carbon dioxide, other gases, water vapour
5	Jupiter	Hydrogen, clouds of ammonia and sulphur
6	Saturn	Hydrogen and helium, ammonia clouds
7	Neptune	Poisonous methane
8	Uranus	Poisonous methane
9	Pluto	Mixture of nitrogen and methane

▲ *All the planets*
are held in their
orbits around the
Sun by the Sun's
gravitational force.
Planets also have
their own gravity.
The bigger the
planet, the bigger its
gravitational pull.
This means that an
astronaut on Jupiter
would weigh 2.5
times as much as a
person on Earth.

» ORBIT ROUND THE SUN

	PLANET	YEARS	DAYS
1	Pluto	248	0
2	Neptune	164	298
3	Uranus	84	4
4	Saturn	29	168
5	Jupiter	11	314
6	Mars	0	687
7	Earth	0	365
8	Venus	0	225
9	Mercury	0	88

Note: Years = Earth years, days = Earth days

OTHER SOLAR SYSTEMS?

● The distant star Upsilon Andromedae is 44 light years away from Earth. It has three planets circling it.

● One of Upsilon Andromedae's three planets is four times bigger than Jupiter.

● About 20 planets have been found orbiting other stars. But the Upsilon Andromedae solar system is the only other solar system spotted so far.

EARTH AND ITS NEIGHBOURS

Earth and its three nearest neighbours, Mercury, Venus and Mars, are all rocky planets. All three are smaller than Earth. There are also at least 5,000 known 'minor planets' or asteroids that orbit the Sun between Mars and Jupiter. Most asteroids are very small. The biggest, named Ceres, is only 930 km in diameter. It is unlikely that Earth's neighbouring planets have life on them, but there is evidence that water once flowed on Mars.

VENUS AND MERCURY

● Although Venus is the brightest of Earth's neighbours, its surface is hidden by clouds.
● Venus is the hottest planet, but Mercury is closer to the Sun.
● Mercury is only slightly bigger than the Moon. In Mercury's sky the Sun looks twice as big as it does from Earth.

▼ Asteroids are huge lumps of rock that orbit between Mars and Jupiter. The biggest is Ceres at 930 km in diameter. Astronomers think there may be millions of asteroids in space.

›› PLANET STATISTICS

	PLANET	MASS	DIAMETER
★ 1	Earth	1	1
2	Venus	0.8	0.9
3	Mars	0.1	0.5
4	Mercury	0.05	0.3

Note: Figures are comparisons with Earth. Earth = 1

▲ *Asteroids crossing Earth's path hit the surface as meteorites. Thousands of meteorites hit each year, but giants are very rare.*

DID YOU KNOW?

The mass (weight) of Earth is about 6 x 21 zeros. Written out it looks like this: 6,000,000,000,000,000,000,000 tonnes. It's quicker to say Earth weighs about 6 sextillion tonnes.

▲ *Mountains rise over Venus, where temperatures can reach almost 500°C. Sulphuric acid rains down and the surface pressure is similar in strength to the water pressure on Earth's ocean beds.*

◄ *Mars is known as the red planet because of its red-brown soil. At 27 km high, its highest mountain, an extinct volcano called Olympus Mons, is three times higher than Mount Everest.*

4   2   1   3

GIANT PLANETS

The four biggest planets in the Solar System are the ringed 'gas giants': Jupiter, Saturn, Uranus and Neptune. These are the four planets farthest from the Sun, apart from Pluto. The orbits that they make around the Sun are not perfect circles, but are 'elliptical'. This means that each planet's distance from the Sun varies during one orbit. The best time to see the outer planets is when they are closest to Earth and opposite the Sun.

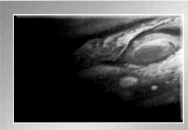

DID YOU KNOW?
The Great Red Spot visible on the surface of Jupiter is a huge storm – a giant gas hurricane as big as two Earths.

Jupiter

Saturn

▲ *Jupiter is a ball of gases, mostly hydrogen and helium. Spinning faster than any other planet, the clouds in its atmosphere are whipped up into vast, swirling storms with winds of up to 500 km/h. Jupiter has the shortest day of all the planets. A day on Jupiter lasts just under 10 hours (9 hours 55 minutes).*

▲ *Saturn is the second biggest gas giant. This planet's rings are one of the most spectacular sights in the Solar System. Measuring 270,000 km from edge to edge, they are made up of millions of whirling blocks of ice. Saturn spins almost as fast as Jupiter, and is colder and even windier, with storm winds ten times faster than a hurricane on Earth.*

▶ *In 1995 the little* Galileo *space probe reached Jupiter on its mission to photograph the planet. The probe was named after Galileo Galilei, who in 1609 was the first person to see Jupiter's moons (he spotted four). After entering Jupiter's atmosphere, the* Galileo *probe survived an hour in the stormy, freezing clouds before it was crushed and vaporized.*

▼ *Uranus is a blue-green world of freezing chemical slush shrouded in clouds of methane gas and tilted on its side. It was discovered in 1781 by William Herschel – the first person in recorded history to find a new planet. Uranus has at least 21 moons, possibly more.*

▼ *Neptune is almost four times larger than Earth. Scientists believe that, like Uranus, it is a sea of liquid methane surrounding a core of rock. The Great Dark Spot on its surface is a huge, rotating storm bigger than Earth. Neptune is 30 times farther than Earth is from the Sun.*

Uranus

Neptune

JUPITER AND THE SUN

● Jupiter is so big that 1,000 Earths would fit inside it.
● The Sun is so much bigger than Jupiter that 900 Jupiters would fit inside the Sun.
● There are stars 2,000 times bigger than the Sun. Mind-boggling!

▶▶	THE FOUR GIANT PLANETS	
	PLANET	VOLUME
★ 1	Jupiter	1,300
2	Saturn	766
3	Uranus	63
4	Neptune	58
Note: Volumes are compared with Earth. Earth = 1		

MOONS

Moons are satellites that are held in orbit around planets. Earth has one satellite, the Moon, which is a lump of rock about as wide as Australia. Earth weighs as much as 81 Moons! An astronaut can jump six times higher on the Moon than on Earth, but because the Moon has no air, a human cannot walk there without a spacesuit and life-support system. There are many other moons in the Solar System, some of them much bigger than our Moon.

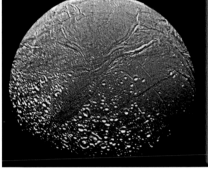

▲ Saturn has 18 known moons. One of them is the small, 500-km-wide moon called Enceladus, shown here. It glistens as light reflects off beads of ice on the surface. Enceladus is unusual in having deep valleys, which indicate geological activity.

▲ The Moon spins on its axis in 27.3 days – the same amount of time it takes to complete one orbit of Earth.

▸▸ THE MOST MOONS		
PLANET		**NUMBER OF MOONS**
1	Uranus	21
2	Saturn	18
3	Jupiter	16
4	Neptune	8
5	Mars	2
6	Earth	1
7	Pluto	1
8	Venus	0
8	Mercury	0

▼ From samples brought back by astronauts, scientists learned that the top soil of the Moon is just dust, firm enough to support a spacecraft. They think the rocks may contain water, which would be useful for a future Moon base. Astronauts in the 1970s used a Lunar Rover, or Moon buggy, to explore the Moon's surface.

Europa
3,126 km in diameter

Io
3,632 km in diameter

Callisto
4,820 km in diameter

Ganymede
5,276 km in diameter

▲ *The four biggest of Jupiter's 16 moons are all bigger than Pluto. Ganymede is the biggest in the Solar System, Callisto has the most craters, Io has the most volcanoes and Europa is encased in ice.*

▸▸ FACTS ABOUT THE MOON

Distance from Earth	**384,399 km (average)**
Diameter	**3,476 km**
Biggest crater (far side)	**South Pole-Aitken: 2,500 km across, 12,000 m deep**
Biggest crater (visible from Earth)	**Bailly: 295 km across, 4,250 m deep**
Highest mountains	**8,000 m, near the Korolev Basin on the far side**
Length of day/night	**Roughly 15 Earth days each**
Coldest time	**Night: temperatures fall to -163°C**

▲ *Triton, the biggest of Neptune's eight moons, is gradually spiralling towards Neptune and in 10 million to 100 million years time will break up and form rings round the planet. Triton's geysers shoot out frozen nitrogen gas.*

IT'S A FACT
There is no wind or rain on the Moon, so any mark made in the powdery dust stays intact. Footprints left by the Apollo *astronauts will last for thousands of years – unless a meteorite hits them!*

SHOOTING STARS

Millions of meteors whizz through space all the time. Meteors are pieces of dust or lumps of rock from the tails of comets. When they hit Earth's thick atmosphere they heat up and for a second or two trail glowing tails before burning up. These brief flashes, like brilliant fireworks, are called shooting stars. A large meteor sometimes hurtles through Earth's atmosphere and smashes into the ground. The charred rock that remains is called a meteorite.

▲ *The Hoba meteorite was found in Namibia, southern Africa, in 1920. It is big enough for a football team to sit on.*

▲ *A meteor shower is a dramatic display of shooting stars. For a short period more than a thousand a second may flash across the sky. August is the best month to see one.*

BIGGEST METEORITES TO HIT EARTH		
NAME	**COUNTRY**	**WEIGHT**
1 Hoba	Namibia	54 tonnes
2 Campo del Cielo	Argentina	41 tonnes
3 Ahnighito	Greenland	31 tonnes

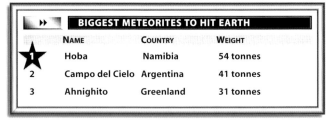

▼ *The most famous hole made by a meteorite is Meteor Crater in Arizona, USA, shown here. It measures more than 1,700 m across and nearly 200 m deep. An even bigger impact crater, partly beneath the sea, is the Chixulub Basin in Mexico, which is 300 km across. This hole was probably made by an asteroid hitting Earth about 65 million years ago – the impact may have wiped out the dinosaurs.*

DID YOU KNOW?
A comet that appeared in 1064 – probably Halley's – is shown in the Bayeux Tapestry, which records William of Normandy's successful invasion of England in 1066.

◀ *In medieval times people thought the fiery tail of a comet was a bad omen, foretelling disaster. Now we know that comets orbit the Sun just like planets, and return on schedule. Halley's Comet comes close to Earth roughly every 77 years.*

THE TALE OF HALLEY'S COMET

1064	The comet was later recorded in the Bayeux Tapestry
1705	Edmund Halley calculated the orbit took 76 to 77 years
1758	Great excitement: the comet returned as Halley predicted
1835	The comet was seen, but it was not as bright as before
1910	Many people feared the world would end
1986	Several spacecraft flew close to the comet
2062	This is the next time Halley's Comet will return

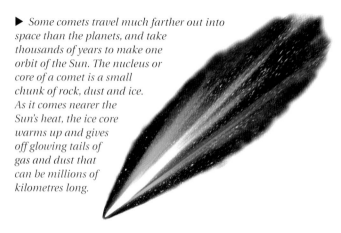

▶ *Some comets travel much farther out into space than the planets, and take thousands of years to make one orbit of the Sun. The nucleus or core of a comet is a small chunk of rock, dust and ice. As it comes nearer the Sun's heat, the ice core warms up and gives off glowing tails of gas and dust that can be millions of kilometres long.*

▲ *The Hale-Bopp Comet was spotted by two astronomers hundreds of kilometres apart on the same night in 1995, so it was named after both of them. It made a spectacular display in March 1997, and will come close to Earth again in about 2,380 years time!*

SPOT THE COMET

● You don't have to wait 77 years for Halley's Comet to see a comet. Others are visible from Earth much more frequently.

● Comet Encke returns every 3 years.

● Comet Grigg-Skjellerup returns every 4 years. In 1992 the *Giotto* space probe flew within 200 km of its nucleus.

● Biela's Comet can be seen every 6.7 years.

STAR GAZING

About 1,900 years ago the Greek astronomer Ptolemy counted 1,080 stars. Like all astronomers of the ancient world, he had no telescope. The Egyptians, Babylonians, Chinese and Greeks all studied the night sky. They named the five planets they could see, and also gave names to the stars. People in ancient times believed gods lived among the stars. They built temples to line up with the positions of bright stars or with the Sun and Moon, and set up stone circles to mark sunrise and sunset on the longest and shortest days in the year.

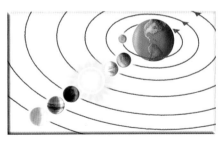

▲ *In ancient times people believed the view of the great classical thinker, Ptolemy, that Earth was at the centre of the Universe and that the heavens moved around Earth. This view was widely accepted for 2,000 years, until Copernicus dared to disagree.*

▶ *The first simple telescope – two lenses held in line – was invented in 1608. The following year, Galileo Galilei became the first person to use a telescope to study the Sun, Moon and planets. He observed that the Sun was not perfect, as people believed, but that it had spots! By the 1700s astronomers were building huge telescopes.*

»	EARLIEST ASTRONOMERS	
	WHO	**WHEN**
1	**Chinese**	1300s BC
2	**Pythagoras**	569–475 BC
3	**Aristarchus**	310–230 BC
4	**Eratosthenes**	c.270–190 BC
5	**Copernicus**	AD 1473–1543

▶ *The world's biggest optical telescope is the Keck Telescope in Hawaii. It has 36 mirrors, each 1.8 m wide. Using lasers, the mirrors are adjusted to act as one giant mirror, four times more powerful than the Mount Palomar telescope in California, USA.*

▲ *Radio waves from space were discovered by Karl Jansky in 1931. The biggest radio telescope is in New Mexico, USA. Called the Very Large Array (VLA), it has 27 dishes, each measuring 25 m across.*

▼ *The Hubble Space Telescope, which was launched in 1990, weighs 11 tonnes and has a 240-cm mirror. Orbiting above Earth's polluted atmosphere, it gives astronomers a clear view of the stars.*

ACHIEVEMENT

Drew maps of the stars and constellations

Declared that Earth was round

Proved the Sun was farther away from Earth than the Moon

Calculated the size of Earth using geometry

Explained how the planets move around the Sun

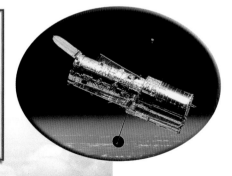

◀ *Stonehenge is the most famous ancient monument in Britain. It was built between about 2950 and 1500 BC. The huge stones were put up in stages, in three circles that made a giant calendar. This was used to fix the days for religious ceremonies, which were linked to the Sun's movement.*

SPACE RACE

French writer Jules Verne wrote about a voyage to the Moon in 1873, and in the 1920s Robert Goddard of the USA launched small home-made rockets. These dreamers were the pioneers of space travel. The space race began in earnest in the 1950s with a contest to put people into orbit around Earth. The Russians won this race. They had the biggest rockets and were able to launch much heavier spacecraft than the Americans. The first big Soviet rocket sent Yuri Gagarin into space in 1961.

▶ SATELLITE LAUNCHES		
	COUNTRY	YEAR
1	USSR	1957
2	USA	1958
3	France	1965
4	Japan	1970
5	China	1970
6	UK	1971

▶ *Soviet cosmonaut Yuri Gagarin was the first person in space. On April 12, 1961, in the 5 tonne spaceship Vostok 1, he made a complete circuit of Earth in just 1 hour and 29 minutes.*

◀ *In 1957 the Russians took the lead in the space race with the first artificial satellite, Sputnik 1. Not much bigger than a beach ball, it contained a radio transmitter.*

▼ *The two* Pioneer *space probes launched by the USA in 1972 and 1973 were the first space probes to head for the outer planets. They flew past Jupiter and Saturn.*

▲ *The Russians dreamed of space travel as early as the 1890s, when Konstantin Tsiolkovski drew plans for building space rockets.*

» THE FIRST SATELLITES

	SATELLITE	COUNTRY	LAUNCH DATE
★1	Sputnik 1	USSR	October 1957
2	Sputnik 2	USSR	November 1957
3	Explorer 1	USA	February 1958
4	Vanguard 1	USA	March 1958

FAST AS LIGHT

● If you could travel at light-speed, like the Millennium Falcon in the film *Star Wars*, you would reach the Moon in under 2 seconds, Pluto in 6 hours, and you would cross the Milky Way in 100,000 years.

▼ *Laika, a fox terrier dog, was the first animal to travel in space. In 1957 she spent a week in orbit aboard the Russian craft Sputnik 2. The Russians knew that they would not be able to bring Laika back, and she died when her oxygen ran out.*

▲ American Neil Armstrong (left) was the first person on the Moon. He took his "giant leap for mankind" on July 20, 1969. Apollo 11's other crew were Edwin 'Buzz' Aldrin (right) and Michael Collins (centre).

◄ *In 1972* Pioneer 10 *was the fastest craft ever launched into space. It left Earth at more than 51,000 km/h on its mission to the outer planets. In 1983 it became the first human-made object to leave the Solar System, and it is now about 11 billion km away!*

▼ *Space races of the future are likely to focus on trying to colonize other planets. This artist's impression is of a futuristic settlement on Mars, where buildings would need their own air supply.*

▲ *The Americans caught up with their rivals with their* Apollo *Moon landers and then the Space Shuttle. Today Russians, Americans and other nations are working together in space.*

GREAT JOURNEYS

Rocket building became a very expensive contest between the Russians and the Americans in the 1960s. Space scientists from both countries borrowed ideas from the Germans, whose V2 rocket of World War II was the first big, long-range rocket. The first big Soviet rocket, *Vostok 1*, put Yuri Gagarin into space. But this was followed by an even bigger rocket, *Saturn 5*, from the Americans. This sent astronauts to the Moon. In the 1980s probes travelled across the Solar System to send back the first close-up pictures of Jupiter and Saturn, and explore the even more distant planets, Uranus and Neptune.

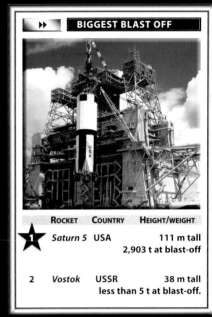

➤➤ BIGGEST BLAST OFF

ROCKET	COUNTRY	HEIGHT/WEIGHT
⭐1 *Saturn 5*	USA	111 m tall 2,903 t at blast-off
2 *Vostok*	USSR	38 m tall less than 5 t at blast-off.

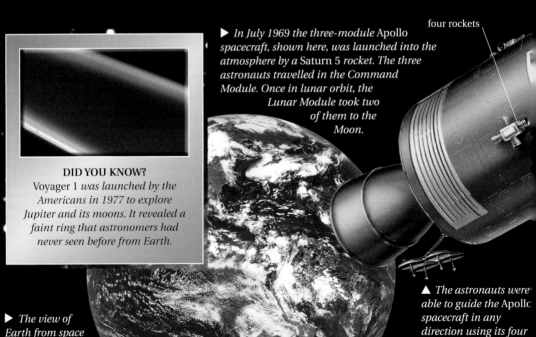

four rockets

▶ *In July 1969 the three-module* Apollo *spacecraft, shown here, was launched into the atmosphere by a* Saturn 5 *rocket. The three astronauts travelled in the Command Module. Once in lunar orbit, the Lunar Module took two of them to the Moon.*

DID YOU KNOW?
Voyager 1 *was launched by the Americans in 1977 to explore Jupiter and its moons. It revealed a faint ring that astronomers had never seen before from Earth.*

▶ *The view of Earth from space has only been seen by humans for just over 40 years!*

▲ *The astronauts were able to guide the* Apollo *spacecraft in any direction using its four thrusters, each with fou rockets pointing in different directions.*

MISSION FIRSTS

Luna 9, Surveyor 1	1966	First Moon landing by unmanned spacecraft
Apollo 11	1969	First Moon landing by astronauts
Lunokhod	1970	First Moon robot rover
Galileo craft	1995	First probe to explore Jupiter's atmosphere
Sojourner	1997	First rover to move about another planet

▶ Apollo 11's mission to the Moon covered 1.5 million km and lasted 195 hours.

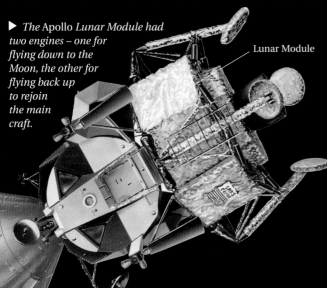

▶ The Apollo *Lunar Module* had two engines – one for flying down to the Moon, the other for flying back up to rejoin the main craft.

Lunar Module

Command Module

▲ Deep space probes such as Voyager 2 travel millions of kilometres from Earth without the use of engines. They send back pictures and other information by radio.

▶ The Americans sent two Viking spacecraft to Mars in 1975. Their mission was to study the planet and look for signs of life. The landers descended from the orbiters to the surface, where they gathered soil samples and took some amazing photographs, but failed to find any Martians!

▲ The Apollo Command Module was the only part of Apollo to return to Earth. The Lunar Module was set adrift once the two astronauts who had taken it to the Moon had returned to the Command Module.

SPACE PROBE FIRSTS

Luna 2	USSR	1959	First to hit the Moon
Luna 3	USSR	1959	First to photograph the Moon's far side
Venera 4	USSR	1967	First to hit Venus
Mars 2 and 3	USSR	1971	First to hit Mars
Viking 1 and 2	USA	1976	First long-stay Mars landing
Pioneer 10	USA	1983	First to leave the Solar System

▼ Apollo 15 *was launched by a* Saturn 5 *rocket from Cape Canaveral, Florida, USA, at 9:34 am on July 26, 1971, just 187 milliseconds behind schedule! The 111-m-high* Saturn 5 *is seen here on the launch pad just before lift-off.*

SPACE MISSIONS

The first astronauts were pilots, trained to fly fast jet planes. An early exception was Valentina Tereshkova, the first woman in space. She was a textile technologist, but also an expert parachutist. Later astronauts included scientists and doctors, as well as a geologist on *Apollo 17*. By the 1980s astronauts had proved people could stay in space for up to a year without harming their bodies or going mad. There have been some tragedies, however, and at least one near-disaster. Space can be a dangerous and hostile place.

▲ Apollo 15's *Lunar Module*, Falcon, *took two astronauts to the Moon's surface. There, for the first time, they used the Lunar Rover or Moon buggy to travel about. The crew proudly left the US flag standing in the Moon's dust before they left for home.*

►►	ASTRONAUT FIRSTS		
Gherman Titov	USSR	1961	First day in space
Andrian Nikolayev	USSR	1962	First 3-day flight
Valentina Tereshkova	USSR	1963	First woman in space
Voskhod 1	USSR	1964	First 3-person crew
Aleksei Leonov	USSR	1965	First space walk

IT'S A FACT
In 1971 US astronauts David Scott and James Irwin were the first people to drive on the Moon. They rode around in a battery-powered, four-wheeled Moon buggy.

▸▸	**FIRST FIVE PEOPLE IN ORBIT**		
	NAME	**COUNTRY**	**DATE**
★1	Yuri Gagarin	USSR	April 12, 1961
2	Gherman Titov	USSR	August 6–7, 1961
3	John Glenn	USA	February 20, 1962
4	M. Scott Carpenter	USA	May 24, 1962
5	Andrian Nikolayev	USSR	August 11–15, 1962

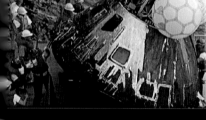

▲ Apollo 13 *limped back to Earth low on power and air after an explosion damaged the main part of the craft. Millions of television viewers held their breath awaiting the return of the three crew.*

▶ *Astronauts do spacewalks to make repairs to their craft or to satellites or space telescopes.*

▸▸	**US MOON MISSIONS AND MOON WALKERS**	Note: *Apollo 9* orbited Earth
Apollo 8	December 1968	Three astronauts flew around the Moon
Apollo 10	May 1969	Flew to within 14 km of the Moon's surface
Apollo 11	July 1969	Neil Armstrong and Edwin Aldrin landed
Apollo 12	November 1969	Pete Conrad and Alan Bean landed
Apollo 13	April 1970	Flew around the Moon
Apollo 14	January 1971	Alan Shepard and Edgar Mitchell landed
Apollo 15	July 1971	David Scott and James Irwin landed
Apollo 16	April 1972	John Young and Charles Duke landed
Apollo 17	December 1972	Harrison Schmitt and Gene Cernan landed

SPACE SHUTTLES

The American Space Shuttle was the world's first reusable spacecraft. It can carry eight astronauts into space, stay in orbit for up to 10 days, and then fly back to land on an airstrip. It can launch satellites from its cargo bay, and bring back faulty ones for repair. Other satellite launchers, such as the European *Ariane* rocket, can be used only once. The Shuttle first flew in 1981, and will be used many times to carry equipment to and from the new International Space Station.

SHUTTLE FACTS

- The Shuttle weighs 2 million kg at lift-off.
- From nose to tail it measures 56 m.
- It orbits at a height of between 200 and 600 km above Earth.
- The four original Shuttles were named *Columbia, Challenger, Discovery* and *Atlantis.*
- In 1991 *Endeavour* replaced *Challenger,* lost in 1986.

▶ *In orbit, circling Earth at a speed of about 28,000 km/h, the Shuttle can launch satellites from its 18-m-long cargo bay, which can carry a load of more than 35 tonnes. The crew use a 'remote manipulator arm' to catch satellites for repair.*

DID YOU KNOW?
Rocket engines burn fuel at an incredible rate. During lift-off the Shuttle burns nearly 10 tonnes of fuel a second from its external fuel tank.

▼ *The winged Space Shuttle lifts off and rides into orbit attached to a giant external fuel tank with boosters either side. In 1986* Challenger *exploded just 72 seconds after lift-off, killing its seven crew.*

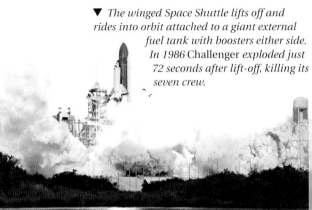

▼ *Shuttle astronauts emerge into the cargo bay wearing spacesuits to work. Their jobs include 'capturing' satellites, which sometimes need repair or new parts.*

▶ *Lift-off! The Shuttle is blasted upwards by its three main engines, aided by the two solid fuel rocket boosters. These burn out after two minutes, at a height of 45 km, and fall back to Earth by parachute to be used again. After eight minutes the external fuel tank, now empty, also falls into the ocean. It too can be reused.*

▼ *When the Shuttle re-enters Earth's atmosphere, it glows red-hot from the heat of friction. Special tiles absorb the heat. It lands on a runway, ready to be used again on another mission.*

▶▶	**SHUTTLE FIRSTS**	
Columbia	1981	**First test flight**
Columbia	1982	**First 4-person flight**
Columbia	1983	**First 5-person flight and first US woman**
Challenger	1984	**First free walk in space using a jet-pack**
Challenger	1985	**First 8-person flight**

SPACE STATIONS

The first space station was *Salyut 1*, launched by the Russians in 1971. A series of *Salyuts* followed before the Russians built the larger *Mir* space station in 1986. *Mir* had six docking ports to which other modules or visiting spacecraft could be attached. In 1995 cosmonaut Valeriy Poliyakov spent 437 days in orbit in *Mir*, setting a space record. Russia and America are now working with Japan, Canada and Europe to build the new *International Space Station (ISS)*.

▲ *Building the* International Space Station *will take over 5 years and will require 45 Shuttle flights. The cost is put at 100 billion US dollars, making it the most expensive object ever built! The* ISS *is being put together in sections. When complete, it will be as big as a football pitch.*

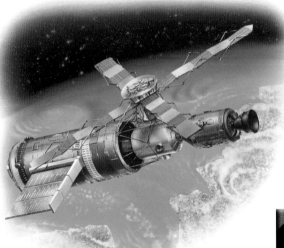

MIR FACTS

● The main section of *Mir* was 13.13 m long, 4.2 m wide and weighed 21 tonnes.
● The *Kvant* module was joined to *Mir* in 1987, doubling the room inside.
● *Kvant 3* (1990) had equipment that turned *Mir* into a space factory.

▲ *The American* Skylab, *launched in 1973, had problems with a solar panel, forcing the crew to put up a 'sunshade' to keep it cool. Despite the snags, three 3-man crews visited* Skylab, *the longest mission lasting 84 days. The 75-tonne space station burned up in the atmosphere in 1979.*

▶ *This artist's impression shows the Shuttle docking with the* International Space Station. *The Shuttle will be used to transport astronauts, equipment, provisions and visitors to the space station once building is complete.*

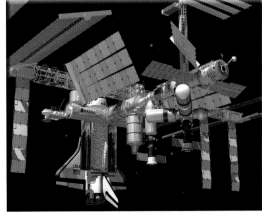

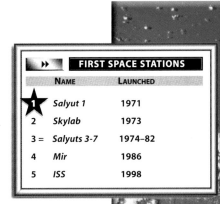

FIRST SPACE STATIONS

	NAME	LAUNCHED
1	**Salyut 1**	1971
2	**Skylab**	1973
3 =	**Salyuts 3-7**	1974–82
4	**Mir**	1986
5	**ISS**	1998

▶ *The Russian space station* Mir, *meaning 'peace', was launched in 1986 to study the long-term effects of living in space. Experiments carried out there included making ultra-pure medicines. Astronauts went on visiting* Mir *until the end of the 1990s, when the ageing space station was finally shut down.*

DID YOU KNOW?
Small 'lifeboat' shuttles like this (the cancelled X–38) could rescue space station crews in future, should things go wrong.

UNIVERSE *QUIZ*

Now that you have read all about what's biggest and best in the Universe, see if you can answer these 20 quiz questions! (Pictures give clues, answers at the top of the page.)

◀ *3. What is the constellation Ursa Major also known as?*

▶ *4. Where is the hottest part of the Sun?*

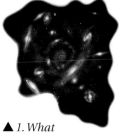

▲ *1. What was the biggest event in the Universe?*

▲ *2. The Milky Way is what type of galaxy?*

▼ *5. Which is the hottest planet?*

▶ *6. How many times could Earth fit into the Sun?*

▶ *7. How long (in hours and minutes) is a day on Jupiter?*

▶ *8. Which planet takes 248 years to orbit the Sun?*

▼ *10. Which scientist claimed that Earth was the centre of the Universe?*

▶ *9. Which planet has thousands of rings?*

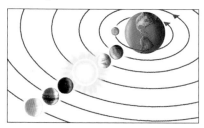

▼ 12. Which planet has a mountain three times higher than Mount Everest?

▲ 11. Which planet is closest to the Sun?

▲ 13. Which famous comet appears in the Bayeux Tapestry?

▼ 14. Who first looked into space through a telescope?

◄ 15. What was the name of the first animal in space?

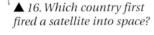

▲ 16. Which country first fired a satellite into space?

◄ 19. How fast does the Space Shuttle orbit Earth?

▲ 17. Which was the biggest rocket ever built?

▲ 18. Who were the first two men on the Moon (shown on the left and the right)?

◄ 20. How big is the International Space Station?

INDEX

Entries in bold refer to illustrations

*The publishers wish to thank the following artists
who have contributed to this book:*

Rob Jakeway, Kuo Kang Chen, Alan Male, Janos Marffy, Peter Sarson,
Mike White/Temple Rogers

*The publishers wish to thank the following sources for the
photographs used in this book:*

CORBIS: Page 25 (T/R) Roger Ressmeyyer; Page 30 (L);
Page 31 (T/L) NASA
Klaus G. Hinkelmann: Page 22 (T/R)
All other photographs from Miles Kelly Archives and NASA